Self Help for the Would-Be Blogger

The Why's and How's of Blogging for People Who Don't Blog

Written by

Judy Wesener

Copyright 2010

It is common sense to take a method and try it. If it fails, admit it frankly and try another. But above all, try something.- Franklyn Roosevelt

This book is dedicated to all you would-be bloggers out there! Wishing you the best of luck and, above all, *HAVE FUN!*

Table of Contents

Preface

If you've never blogged, but have wondered what it's all about, than this is the book for you. It's written in plain English, none of that techy stuff, (well, very little of it anyhow). After you've finished reading, you should be able to determine which type of blog is best for you and how to get started. You'll also have a basic understanding of what blogging is all about and what it may mean to you, your business, and/or your charitable cause.

I've tried to present a broad overview of the blogosphere (this is a term used to reference blogs and their interconnections within a connected community or a social network). I've included information on different blogging methods ranging from text blogs to video blogs.

At the time of this writing, the information contain here is current and relevant. However, the web changes quickly, for that reason I've suggested numerous times throughout the book to do a search on google, Yahoo, or your search engine of choice, for the most up-to-date information or websites available to suit your needs. New websites appear daily and may be a valuable resource for you.

You'll be given information on different types of blogs, so you can decide which blogging method might best suite your needs. I've also included a short list of ideas to help get you started. Don't ever think you have nothing to contribute. Everyone has interests, hobbies or knowledge they can share with others. There are other people out there in the world who would love to hear what you have to say.

You'll learn several ways to drive traffic to your blog, many of which you can use right away; as well as simple tips you can implement for improving your search engine rankings. This will be especially important if you plan to blog for a cause or in order to promote your business or online product.

There's even a section suggesting several ways your blog can make you money, however, these methods work best after you've has built up a good blog following.

This book also touches on some more advanced techniques; however, this is just to make you aware that they exist. I don't go into a lot of detail on some of these techniques, when you find yourself ready to take the next step, there are many books out there ready to teach you advanced methodology. You can also find information on many of the advanced steps, by doing a search for the specific topic on the web.

My goal in creating this book was to get you started blogging, not overwhelm you. Many people start out by diving into something that is beyond their current skill level or knowledge, they find themselves overwhelmed and give up. Just jump in, get your feet wet and move forward at your own pace.

What is a blog anyway?

The word blog came initially from the term weblog. A blog is essentially an online journal in which you write down your ideas, opinions, thoughts or whatever information you'd like to share with other people.

Always keep in mind that with a blog, you aren't just communicating information to your readers, you're creating a community. This community consists of visitors who join your feed and will continue to come back to your blog on a regular basis.

You'll find numerous free blogging sites. It's very easy to become a member of one of these blogging website. Find a site where you'd like your blog to appear, register, customize your template and you're ready to start. Once you've registered and become a member, you're automatically a part of a specific blogging community. You may want to start by spending some time browsing through other blogs on the site. In this way, you'll be able to get some ideas for the type of information you'd like to post in your own blog.

When you post a blog, you pick the style, format, and settings you want to use to convey your thoughts, opinions or messages. Blogging sites offer a variety of features to enhance your blog, such as templates, hyperlink, plain text, pictures, video and audio. A number of blogging sites enable you to upload video and audio on your blogs, creating excitement and appeal for your visitors. Just a note here, be sure your visitors have control over all video and audio. They need to be able to start and stop it for themselves.

Blogging has very few, if any, rules and is popular worldwide. Just remember search engines will pick up your blog and anyone in the world can see what you've written. Words, whether spoken or written, can have legal repercussions. You never know who will read what you've posted, so keep that fact in mind when you write and post something on the Internet.

Many bloggers are now creating audio blogs. This method uses the spoken word to produce entries instead of writing text. This popular method can also include text, making them search engine friendly. Video blogging is becoming very popular, as well. With this method, you create and upload videos to your blog. There are many programs available to make this process easier. With all the portable web friendly devices available, this method is growing in popularity.

Successful Blogging

People may choose to start and maintain a blog for any number of reasons. Whether you want to generate revenue, keep up with family members and friends or provide useful information to the public, this can be the perfect venue for you.

Starting a personal blog is the easiest way to begin. You may want to start with this type of blog just to get the feel for blogging and how it works. Free Blogging Websites provide templates for you to use. Be sure to check them out to determine which one might work best for you. They're very easy to set up and you could easily have your blog online in less than 1 hour.

If your desire is to create revenue through blogging, it's wise to spend a little time doing some initial research. Just like many other things in life, doing a little research before you begin can pay off big in the long run. You don't want to make mistakes at the very beginning that can prove to be detrimental to your success. Two great methods include using the Internet to research blogging and reading successful blogs in your niche.

Choosing Your Blog Topic

Ideally, it would be wise for you to choose subject matter with which you're both knowledgeable and passionate. You'll need to have a clear purpose in mind, before you begin blogging. Carefully consider the subject matter for your blog, before you begin. This becomes even more important if your purpose is to make money. If your blog is being created for financial reasons, it's important to consider other blogs within your same niche. Can you compete with these blogs without copying their content? If not, you may want to rethink your niche or maybe even find a niche within a niche.

Finding Your Niche

- What interests you?
- Playing Xbox
- Pets
- Camping
- Hiking
- Fishing
- Hunting
- Playing or Watching Sports
- Gardening
- Travel
- Children or Grandchildren
- Do you have a hobby?
- Motorcycling

- Gardening
- Scrapbooking
- Beading
- Ceramics
- Cooking
- Woodworking
- Video Gaming
- Movie Buff
- Ways to Save Money

The ideas are endless.

Where does your passion lie? What gets you excited? Are you an expert on any particular subject? Are you learning something new that you'd like to share with others?

Everyone has something to share. We all have experience or knowledge of interest to others. Even is you're a couch potato, you can blog about your favorite television programs or movies. You aren't the only one watching them.

It's important that your visitors sense your passion for the subject you choose. They also expect to see knowledgeable and informative posts, containing information that is both accurate and interesting. Besides, you'll find it much easier to come up with new and interesting, if you have some type of solid foundation in mind for your blog.

You can choose to write your blog about widely popular topics, if you like, but remember there is an audience out there for even the most obscure subjects. People are interested in a wide range of topics. If you're planning on using your blog to promote a website or for making money, it would be more beneficial to blog on topics of interest to a larger audience. You would need to develop a large reader base in order to promote a website or create income. But if it's more for personal purposes, you can certainly blog about a little known subject that's of interest to you.

Evaluating Other Blogs in Your Niche

After you've selected a topic, you may want to consider checking out the other bloggers who share your interest and have already been writing on your chosen subject. This is a perfect way of evaluating whether your subject has already reached its saturation point. It's very difficult for a new blogger to get the traffic they need in a saturated market, this is especially important if the purpose of your blog is to create an income.

Looking at the existing blogs, on your subject matter, will give you the opportunity to check out the quality of the blogs and whether or not you feel you'll be able to compete with existing blogs for visitor traffic.

The world is full of interesting information you can put into a blog, incase you decide to rethink you topic. Remember, a broad topic will contain many subtopics. Maybe blogs about football have already saturated the market, but what about a blog about tailgate parties, or specifics about your favorite team?

So if blogs for your chosen topic, have already saturated the blogspere, don't give up. Brainstorm subtopics on your topic, you may come up what the perfect idea for your blog.

Deciding on The Best Free Blogging Site

It can be very overwhelming when you begin looking for the blogging site that best suites you and your interests. Many sites are very large and well established, such as Blogger, but there's also a wide selection of smaller sites.

You may want to choose a large, established site if reliability is a concern, especially if your blogging for business reasons. When choosing a well-established site, you'll have the security of knowing your blog won't crash at the worst possible time, or worse yet, disappear altogether. Large, well-established sites will most probably be more reliable.

Many bloggers choose smaller, newer sites for a variety of personal reasons. You can check out both types, to decide on which type is the best fit for you and your needs.

Examples of Free Blogging Sites:

- Blogger.com
- Wordpress.com
- Myblogsite.com
- LiveJournal.com
- Blogspot.com

This list is just the tip of the iceberg (so to speak). The blogging site you choose is completely a personal preference. It's about what feels right for you. Spend a little time checking them out and see which one suits your style and needs.

The 4 Basic Parts of a Blog

Title – Make your title as descriptive as possible, but try to keep it between 6 – 8 words. It's important to grab perspective readers' attention quickly. You want the search engines to pick it up and display it in search results. You don't want your reader wondering what the blog is about; make your title concise. The whole point of your blog is to get them to click on it and read what you've posted.

"How To" titles get attention. Look at magazines, what words did they use to make you want to read an article? They've been grabbing reader attention for years. Follow what's been proven to work. Use the same technique to bring readers to your blog.

Specialized blogs are very popular. Many blogs follow a topic such as: politics, sports, philosophy, social commentary, even pet care and gardening. These blogs promote their specific themes, giving people a means to share knowledge and opinions with others who share their passion.

Text Box – This is where your going to actually type in your text, post links, pictures, audio, video and more. Keep your posts short and concise, 350 – 500 words is best.

By using images, subheadings, lists and bullets, you'll be able to catch and keep your readers attention. Ask questions to create interaction with your viewers.

Comments –Your readers can (and will) leave remarks regarding your post. They may ask a question, provided additional information or simply leave a comment. It's important to welcome these comments and create an atmosphere of open communication to bring your viewer back and create a community.

Tags – This is where you type in keywords relating to your blog entry. Keywords are words or phrases related to the content of your post. It's a serious mistake to not use well-chosen keywords and phrases on your blog because search engine spiders depend on these to find you. It's very difficult to find your blog on the web without concise keywords. This is especially critical if you're promoting a business or product on your blog.

You may hear the term trackback in reference to blogging. Simply put, trackback (refers to any type of linkback) is an acknowledgement, primarily used for communication between blogs. This allows readers of several blogs to follow the conversations.

When you create your blog template, make sure the RSS feed sign-up box is in a prominent place. You want your visitors to notice it right away and become subscribers to your blog, thus creating continued traffic to your blog posts.

Unlike, websites, which have several distinct pages, most blogs, have simple templates with an area for your title, text body, category, tags, etc. By using the templates offered by the blogging site, you can start your blog right away; this is especially handy for first time users. There are many great free templates available, which you can customize by adding a logo, picture or changing the color scheme.

Try out the free templates and services offered by the blogging website you choose, before you opt to pay for a special templates or extra services. Unlike websites, you won't need to pay for hosting service fees or domain names with a blog.

Typical Blogging Formats

Regardless of your reason for starting a blog, it's a wonderful way to interact with people. You'll meet people who share your interests and want to discuss them with you.

By far, using Blog Directories is the quickest way to find blogs that may interest you. If you're a first time user, you'll be able to gain valuable insight into the blogging world by browsing through these directories. This will also give you ideas for your own blog.

Personal Blogs

Many bloggers create personal journals (blogs) to document their day-to-day activities. They keep their readers posted on the events happening in their lives. Many times you'll find people who post short stories, or poems, which they've either written themselves or are by someone they admire.

This is the type of blog you'll find most often and is very popular in the blogging world. It's definitely the easiest type for the first time blogger. Individuals, who wish to post poems, rants and opinions, can easily find an audience through blogging.

If you've never blogged before, you may want to try your hand with a personal blog first. This will give you a chance to "get your feet wet", so to speak and do some experimenting with blog templates and writing styles.

Business Blogs

Blogging isn't limited to personal usage. More and more savvy large businesses and entrepreneurs are using blogging to promote their businesses. This is a perfect way to be found on the web and bring new customers to your website or other selling platforms.

Many people promote their online businesses and merchandise through blogging. With millions of people logging onto the Internet everyday, blogging has become a profitable and relativity easy way to promote almost any type of business.

Business blogs are an effective way to allow your customers to "get to know" you. This helps to put them at ease and to alleviate the apprehension of dealing with a stranger who may be less than honest.

Educational Blogs

A number of Universities, and other types of schools, are now posting educational blogs. They post information concerning lessons or lesson plans. This now allows students to ask questions or provide input. Using this digital form of communications allows students who have missed classes, or may be need additional information, to easily find their assignments and ask questions. Educational blogs are very popular for instructors teaching online classes.

Educational Blogs help to add a personal touch to the online learning experience. Many students appreciate this extra attention.

Blogging for a Cause

As a Blogger, you have the ability to change the world with your words. You can use those words to promote your favorite charitable cause. Make a difference! If there's something that's really dear to your heart, you may want to create a blog to bring your worthwhile cause to the world.

One thing that's really important is that your blog have a logo or banner with the name of your cause. This should be prominent and obvious to anyone visiting. You can place a picture of the cause logo or create a logo with a link, where people can learn more or make a donation.

Be passionate when you write about your charitable cause or causes. Your goal is to make your reads feel your passion and join you. Be consistent and keep your follower updated on all future activities and functions related the your cause.

With the advances in web technologies, and personal web devices, bloggers can add audio and video to create an interesting blog experience for their audience. The use of mobile devices has made it much easier to update your blog on the run. Blogging events as they happen, instead of waiting to return to your computer to make your updates.

Blogging is fun and perfect for nearly everyone. To start, all you need to do is type Blogging Sites into any search engine. Then just start checking them out to see what will work best for you!

Tips for Blog Designs and Layouts that POP!

Although writing a blog with interesting and up-to-date content is extremely important, design and layout should not be overlooked. Your blogs design and layout needs to grab your visitors' interest. By following a few simple design tips, you can make your blog stand out in the crowd, and believe me, there's a lot of blogs out there; you do want to stand out!

Add a Favicon

The word favicon is short for "favorites icon". Simply put, it's an icon created as a website or URL icon, also for bookmarks or shortcuts. OK, so what exactly is it anyway? A favicon is the symbol that appears in the website address bar in front of the URL. For example, if you type google in the address bar, when the google page loads, you'll see google's logo in front of the http://. Favicons will display in the address bar of all modern browsers.

Adding a favicon will give your blog a polished and professional look. There are many websites that will allow you to create a favicon at no cost to you. When you're ready to do this, just type Favicon into any web browser. You'll find plenty of websites offering tools for making your own favicon, there are also sites offering to make one for you, at a cost, of course. Depending on your time availability or skill level, you may find having someone make you a favicon is more cost effective. But if you have the time, try making one for yourself by using the free tools offered on the web.

Create a Custom Banner

Many blogs you'll see use the generic banner provided by the blogging website they've chosen. This is fine for a personal blog, however, if your intent is to make money using your blog, you may want to personalize your banner. You can create your own banner by inserting a graphic or picture, which is the same size as the banner. You will be able to add your blog title to your banner.

Creating your own banner isn't as difficult as you may think and you might want to give it a try. However, if this seems beyond your skill level, don't worry, you can have a banner created for you online for a very minimal charge, usually around $10. You probably even know someone who can make you one.

Customized Photos

You can enhance the appearance of your blog by adding a boarder or frame to your photos before posting them. This simple step can really make your photo's stand out.

You may also want to use photos as part of your template design, this will enhance the appearance of your blog and making it unique.

Adding RSS Feeds

This allows your visitors to follow your blog. RSS (Rich Site Summary) is a format used to deliver changing blog (or web) content. This will allow your visitors to stay informed by giving them the option to retrieve all the information on your latest posts.

Adding Audio or Video

These techniques can make your blog interesting and keep your visitors returning to check for new content. Using streaming radio stations, playlists or mp3 files are all great options for adding audio. Video is a little more involved.

One thing you need to remember here is all audio and video needs to be controlled by the visitor. They need to have the ability to turn it on and off, at will.

Advertisement Banners

When you place these banners on your blog, be sure they're placed strategically. You don't want your visitors to have to sift through a bunch of ad banners just to read your blog. Chances are good, they won't bother, they'll just move on to the next blog that isn't all cluttered up with ad banners and is easier to read.

These simple design features will give your blog a professional look and keep your visitors coming back for more. Each of these features will help to increase your blog traffic.

Don't feel that you have to apply all of these elements at one time. It's perfectly fine to add them one at a time, as you feel comfortable. This is your blog; make it reflect your style and personality.

Tips on Using the Internet to Research Blog Topics

One valuable tool for you to use is Google Alerts (http://www.google.com/alerts/). This handy tool will help you stay up-to-date on your blog topic. You simply enter your keywords and you'll receive updates on blog posts, the latest news and other information related to your niche.

Remember, the Internet is an excellent resource when researching any topic, and blogging is no different.

You'll find numerous articles containing tips on starting, maintaining and optimizing your new blog. Much of this information will be very useful to you and will help you to get off to a good start.

But remember, it is the Internet and everything you read may not be reliable, especially when it comes to tips concerning generating traffic. Be careful about websites offering these "fantastic" programs to generate traffic for you, at a price. Many of them tend to make promises they can't keep. This ends up costing you big bucks and generate very little, if any, quality traffic.

Finding and Reading Successful Blogs

If you're new to the blogging world, you can learn a lot by studying successful blogs. You may want to study blogs on the subject that you find interesting. This will allow you to evaluate how the different blog designs, writing styles, fonts and colors affected your reading experience. Did you enjoy the overall experience or did you sort of skip over it and move on to the next blog? Remember, the way you reacted will be a good indication of what attracts visitors or causes them to move on. Pay close attention to blog designs you find compelling. You may want to incorporate some of the blogs attributes into your own blog. Never copy someone else's blog style, simply use it to give you ideas.

What attacked you to that blog? What made you choose to read one blog and not another? What did they do with their title to grab your attention? Did something make you say "WOW"? Make a note of these things. This will give you an idea how you want your blog to look and what you want to avoid.

Remember these simple style rules:

- It's a good idea not to use more than 3 different font styles
- Use fonts that are easy to read
- Don't using distracting, flashing gifs. They can be very disturbing for many readers. If you must use them, do so sparingly.
- Keep your text readable – don't use a black background with dark or yellow text, it's hard to read and will drive reader away.
- If you're using sound or video, give the reader the option of starting and stopping it.

Writing Content for Your Blog

Whatever topic you choose, do it right! It's important to make sure that people will want to read and share your blog with everyone they know. Hopefully the following tips will help you determine what you need to do to write successful blog content.

Catch the attention of your reader right way with your title, which should be between 8 and 10 words. The title should be concise and descriptive. They need to know your blog contains information they want to read. Also, your first two or three sentences should continue to keep their attention. Start with the good stuff! Maybe ask a question, or make a statement. You may have a lot of valuable information to share with them, but your have to get them to read it first!

There's so much on the web for people to read, if you don't grab their attention immediately, they'll click away from your blog and on to something else. They'll never even get to the substance of your post. You've worked hard putting everything together; don't let them get away before they have the benefit of your experience, commentary or witty repartee.

Be very careful what you've written in the body of the post corresponds to your title. Stay on track. If you start out saying one thing, and end up totally off course in a completely different direction, your reader may get confused. Little side trips are fine, but find your way back to the main topic of the blog before ending your post. Tie it all together for your reader. If you don't, they could decide to look for someone who's more cohesive in their thought processes.

Also, not everyone may have the vocabulary you do. Now is not the time to show off all the "big words" you know. Keep your posts understandable and easy to read. Nothing will drive someone away faster then not having the slightest idea what you're talking about. They aren't going to look up all your fancy words to see what you're trying to tell them. They'll move on and you'll lose them and their friends (because they'll never tell anyone about your blog).

Write in the correct style and vernacular for your audience. If you're writing a blog for professionals, use the terminology they use. If you're writing for the general public, write it in a language style they'll understand easily.

Try to keep your posts between 500 and 800 words. If you find you have more than that to say, save it for the next post.

When you've finished writing your blog, do what you'd do with any written material. Proofread it. Check it over for spelling mistakes and errors in grammar. Yes, many people will notice these errors. It's also a good idea to have friends or family read it. They can provide you with useful feedback and catch mistakes you may have missed.

You may notice, while proofreading your blog, it's hard to understand or the ideas you were hoping to convey, end up sounding complicated. If this is the case, rewrite it to clarify your points. Rewrite it until it's very clear to almost anyone who reads it. Don't allow your audience to be confused. You may understand what you want to say, but they don't, that's why they're reading your blog to begin with (and why having friends or family proofread it is important).

Be sure to break up your text into paragraphs, headers and bullets, if appropriate. One big block of text is very hard to read and reflects a poor writing style. Make sure your blog flows and is easy to read.

Don't ramble; make sure your content is interesting and valuable to your reader. Be concise. Don't overestimate the attention span of your readers.

Use a little humor, if appropriate. This can create interest and make your visitor want to continue reading. Everyone likes to smile once in a while!

Following these tips could very likely help you to create a blog that will bring people back, time and time again.

Blogging Styles that Work

Certain posting styles have been proven to drive traffic to your blog. You'll find many people will bookmark and distribute these blogs to their friends, family and associates. The following methods have been tried and proven.

Creating a List

This technique gives you an easy way to organize your content and present it in a clear manner. Lists are easy to follow and concise. People seem to love them. Think about your niche and write down several points of interest. Now create a top 10, 15, 20 (whatever number you'd like) list related to these points. This method alone will give you interesting material for several posts.

Do an Interview

This can work as a perfect Win/Win situation. What you would need to do is interview someone who has a product or service to offer in your niche. Now you have content for your blog and they received free advertising. You can't go wrong with this method, especially if you have an affiliate link to their website.

Create a "How To" Post

Is there something you know how to do? Well, write a blog explaining to others how they can do the same thing. Now a word of caution here, don't just copy what someone else has posted and call it your own. Firstly, that's called plagiarism. Secondly your reader will probably find the original post and you'll lose your credibility and your readers.

Tell a Great Story

Other people enjoy reading a story about something that's happened to someone else. Maybe they've had something similar happen to them and they can relate. Or you can tell them about something they wish they could do. This type of post can create a lot of comments. Your readers will love sharing their experiences or sympathizing with you.

A couple more great methods to create excitement within your blogging community is to hold a contest for your readers or post a poll. These last two items can easily be added to your regular blog post.

These great methods can create a stir on your blog. Be sure to ask your reader for their input. Audience involvement is important when building your community and to create return visitors. Remember, repeat traffic is the objective.

Dealing with Negativity

At some point, someone is going to leave a disapproving comment on your blog. It doesn't matter what the subject matter is, someone, somewhere is going to have something negative to say. When this happens to you, hopefully the following suggests will help you in dealing with these people and comments.

Criticism from Family and Friends

Unfortunately, family and friends are not always going to be supportive. In the case where the person is a stranger to you, they will just leave a comment or maybe send you an email. However, when that person is a family member or a friend, not only will they leave a comment, but will quite possibly voice these opinions to you in person or on the phone.

This can be a very difficult situation for you. Family and friends may object to the content of your blog for any number of reasons. They may feel the blog is uncomplimentary towards them, or maybe even harmful to you, in some way. Either way, they're going to want you to change the content of your blog.

This leaves you with a couple of potential solutions. You can change the theme of your blog, however in doing this, you may have to give up your vision for the blog. You do have the option of talking to the offended friend or family member. You can explain your perspective on the situation and why it's necessary for you to continue along the path you've chosen for your blog.

You can always change the blog in some basic ways, in order to make them happy. Or you can choose to do nothing. But remember, these are your family and friends; you may not want to alienate them by totally disregarding their feeling on the matter.

Negative Comments Left by Your Visitors

The most common form of disapproval you'll experience will be comments left on your blog. Your visitors may leave a negative comment when responding to a specific blog, or they may disapprove of your blog in general. They could just plain disapprove of your topic. There are also always people who are just plain negative.

Although negative comments can be very disheartening to a new blogger, or any blogger for that matter, there are methods you can use to deal with them.

If your topic is one in which you feel there will be a lot of negative reactions, you can choose not to allow comments to be left at all. This method will definitely eliminate any possible negative comments, but it will also eliminate the ability for your supporters to leave comments.

You can delete the comments you find disagreeable, one at a time, but unless you monitor your blog constantly, other visitors will have the chance to read everything before you have to opportunity to delete them.

If you'd prefer to allow all comments posted on your blog to remain, this could spur more blog activity by other visitors responding to the negative comment, either agreeing or disagreeing with the comment. You do have to option of replying to a negative comment yourself, and may choose to use this method. This gives you the opportunity to post a direct rebuttal, recognizing the criticism and defending your original position. This will also create more blog activity.

Using administrative features you always have the option to block visitors from leaving any further comments on your blog. This is a good alternative when you find yourself in a situation where the blog visitor is simply mean spirited. You may also want to use this feature for visitors who continually leave negative comments. Also, use this option to block visitors who you feel are leaving posts for the purpose of spamming your visitors.

Another good option is to set administrative privileges so that all comments have to be approved by you before they post to your blog. This is a prefect way for you to review the comments when you have time and delete anything you deem as inappropriate or objectionable.

Using this option will insure your readers never see comments you feel are inappropriate or not relevant to the overall theme of your blog.

Legal Problems with Blog Posts

You need to be aware that you can be held liable for defamatory comments made on your blog about another person or company. There is a limit to freedom of speech. Also, copyright laws do pertain to you and your blog. Ignoring these laws can cause legal problems to find their way to you. It's best to be aware of these issues and avoid them right from the very beginning. Remember, it's called the World Wide Web for a reason!

Different Types Blogging Platforms

There are different methods available to host your blog. The most common and easiest to use is the Hosting Blog Provider. This is the best method for new bloggers or for people with limited technical experience. The other methods are mentioned just to provide you with the knowledge that they exist. These other methods are best for experienced people, with at least some knowledge of HTML and blogging software.

Hosting Blog Provider

A Hosting Blog Provider doesn't require you to download and install any special software on your computer. You can sign-up for these sites by filling out a form with the required information. Once this is done, all you need to do is follow the step-by-step instructions on how to customize your page. When you've completed that step, you're ready to start blogging. This is the quickest and easiest type to use, making it perfect for beginners. You aren't required to have any knowledge of HTML (Hypertext Markup Language), CSS or any other technical programs. Set-up is fast and easy.

Stand-Alone Software

Another type of blogging platform requires stand-alone software, which you'll need to download and install on your computer. This software can be free or may require a nominal fee. Using this type of platform allows for the blogger to have more control over their blog designs, making it perfect for bloggers who want to have more freedom when customizing their blogs. You may need to have some technical knowledge or, at the very least, someone who can help you if you run into a problem. You'll also need to have a web host in order to post your blog.

Remote Blogging System

A Remote Blogging System is recommended for users who have advanced knowledge of HTML, CSS, blogging and the Internet. You have the option, with this type of platform, to host your blog on an integrated blog host or on your own domain address. If you choose to use your own domain, you'll need to provide a FTP address, FTP Account User Name and Password to the remote web blog system.

You have the option of starting your blog on one platform and as you gain experience and confidence, you can learn the other platforms and start another blog using one or both of them. This might be something you'd like to check into at some point, once you get comfortable with the whole blogging process.

Types of Blogging Software

Blogging may not be difficult, but there are aspects which can be overwhelming to bloggers without a lot of internet experience.

You'll find many blogging software programs designed for easy use and to simplify the blogging process. Although these programs are designed to be user friendly they can still be overwhelming for someone who has never used this type of software.

There are many blogging software programs designed for easy use. Although these programs are designed to be user friendly they can still be overwhelming for someone who has never used this type of software.

Learning to use the interface can be the most difficult part of the program. When you're ready to take this step, just remember to take your time to learn the program before you move on to the more advanced techniques. If you don't do this, you may get frustrated and give up. Taking it slowly will give you the opportunity to build your confidence and produce some great blogs.

If you're going to pay for a software program, try to get one that has a free trial period. That way you can take it for a test drive and see if it'll suite your needs and you're able to use it easily, before you make your purchase.

Blogging software, Keyword generators and Website design software are just a few of the options available.

Blogging Software

Many of these programs are free and can greatly simplify the blogging process. Many templates are included with this type of software. By using one of these templates and selecting your options, you can have a blog up and running in no time at all.

Keyword Generators

If getting a lot of traffic to your blog is your goal, then you may want to consider using a keyword generating program. These programs assist the blogger in determining which keywords they need to use in their blog.

Not only should your blog contain quality material, but also keywords throughout the blog and in the code can contribute to higher search engine rankings. High search engine ranking can mean high blog traffic.

Internet users rely on search engines to help them in locating blogs or websites which pertain to the keywords they type into the search bar. Keywords bring visitors to your blog or website. It's important for you to use keywords that pertain to your blog content. Keyword spamming will hurt your search engine ranking. You're goal is to try to get to the first or second page of the search results. This is critical if your blog was created to be income producing.

Website Design Software

This is great software for a blogger to use to create an appealing and functional blog. This type of software program is perfect for the blogger who does not have any design experience, but wishes to create a unique blog.

Maintaining Your Blog for Success

Although creating a blog can be quite simple, maintaining it can be a bit of a challenge. In order for your blog to be successful, you must maintain it. Unfortunately, here's no simple formula for this, but posting quality material on a regular basis, writing for your target audience, promoting your blog, and keeping track of the changes you make, can have a profound impact on your success.

Regularly Posting New Entries

Don't ever underestimate the importance of posting new entries on your blog! This is the only way you can create dedicated blog visitors. They need a reason to keep coming back to your blog. When they see your content is relevant to them and that you post quality material on a regular basis, they're likely to return in anticipation of new postings.

Your posts can be lengthy, with in-depth material, but even shorter; quality posts can keep your visitors interested. Blog readers are looking for a degree of substance, so keep the really short posts to a minimum.

If you find you just don't have the time to post in-depth material on a regular basis, then inviting guest bloggers can be the perfect solution for you. Be sure to screen your guest bloggers to ensure they're capable of posting items of interest to your audience and will maintain quality posts.

Know your Audience

Subject matter is very important. Successful blogs will normally focus on a specific niche to draw unique visitors. Posting material related to this niche will keep your audience interested and ensure they'll keep coming back to read more. However, subject matter is not the only important aspect to ensure the success of your blog.

The readability of your blog is important, also. Many of the people visiting your blog may prefer to have the information delivered in a brief and concise manner, while others would prefer to see the information presented with bullet points. Some will even prefer lengthy posts. Provide the information in the manner your particular niche audience would like to see. You may need to look at other successful blogs in your niche to see how they present the information. If you notice many of them use bullet points, then you may want to also use this method.

Affects of Changes Made to Blog

Successful bloggers make changes to their blogs carefully, usually one change at a time. After the change is made, you need to take a little time to evaluate how it affected your blog traffic. Even successful bloggers can fail if they don't assess what the change has done to their traffic.

Also, an important point to make at this time is to read the comments left after making a change. How did your readers react? Do they like it? Has it caused confusion? Should you consider abandoning your recent change and coming up with another idea?

Changes that make sense to you may not make sense to your readers. Pay close attention to what your reading are saying about the change or changes you've made. These people are very important to your success.

Guest Bolger's

There may be times when you really need a guest blogger, or several guest bloggers, in order to continue to keep your content fresh or cover for you if you're going to be away. You may want to set up a certain day each week for your guest bloggers. This way you can notify your visitors of who the guest will be and tell them something about your intended guest blogger. Doing this will create a sense of anticipation with your readers and they'll make a point of coming back just to read the new blog post.

Advertising for Your Guest Blogger

One place you can look for a guest blogger is on Job Boards for freelance writers and bloggers. Experienced bloggers often look for opportunities where they can use their skills and be compensated for their time. When using a Job Board, be very specific when describing the skills set you'll need. Be very detailed as to the length of time the guest will be needed and the subject matter you'd like covered.

Making Your Selection

You'll need to request examples of the perspective bloggers work to assure they have the skill sets necessary to maintain the high quality content your visitors are accustomed to reading.

It's wise to ask the guest blogger for references. You'll need to contact these references to confirm the bloggers ability to complete a project; also to verify reliability, and work ethic. These issues are very important, as you'll need to be able to rely on the guest blogger and be able to relax, knowing they have it covered.

Compensation

Guest bloggers may want to be compensated financially, however oftentimes they'll prefer to have a brief biography at the end of the post. This gives them free advertising. Some may want both financial compensation and free advertising space. Be sure you're both clear on the method of compensation and put it in writing. Be as explicit as possible to avoid any disputes in the future. Have this written document before any content is accepted from your guest blogger.

Search Engine Optimization for Your Blog

Search Engine Optimization is very important to anyone who wishes to bring traffic to his or her blog. You need to be ranked on the search engines in order to achieve success. Basically, all search engines employ some type of algorithm to determine how the results will be displayed on a specific topic. Unfortunately, they don't all use the same algorithm, so you'll need to optimize for as many of them as you can. The following techniques, such as using relevant keywords, image tags and generating backlinks will help to improve your rankings on many search engines.

Using Relevant Keywords

This method is possibly the simplest way to optimize search engine rankings. There are different schools of thought on the effective use of keywords.

Some people believe using keywords in the blog post itself is a sufficient way to gain rakings. Then you have those who are certain you have to create high keyword density to get noticed, while still others many believe low keyword density is the answer.

I'd suggest you try all three and measure the results by doing a search for your blog using keywords. Don't do this search too quickly though, because it does take a while for the search engine spider to find you and rank your blog.

Imagines and Your Search Engine Rankings

Many bloggers believe pictures aren't viewed by search engines, however when the search engine spider crawl the content of your blog, they do read the image tags on your pictures. Therefore it's important to place relevant and accurate keywords in your image tags.

How Backlinks Work

A backlink is an incoming link to a blog or website. Simply put, a backlink is created when a website or blog links to your blog or website.

Search engines will find the link to your content on the other website and it'll follow that link to your website. Google and other search engines assign a page rank to your blog or website based on who is willing to link to you. This is why you want quality links only.

Backlinks create traffic to your content. It allows people visiting another website to click on the link and find your blog. If you have relevant content, this new visitor may start following you.

Many search engines really like backlinks, the number of backlinks a blog has helps determine its ranking. A backlink is considered relevant if both sites have content geared toward the same topic, i.e. keywords.

The algorithms of a specific search engine will look at the number of backlinks pointing to a blog or website, as well as the quality of blogs and websites where the backlink were posted. What that means to you is that you want websites or blogs, contain quality content related to your niche or topic, to be linked to you. This will give you a higher ranking within many search engines.

Backlinks to Avoid

- **Link Farms** –A link farm is a group of websites all linking to each other with the intention of increasing their search engine rankings. Google is not only made up of computers, but also talented people. Between the two, they're pretty capable of detecting link farms and punishing the offenders. You may want to avoid backlinks from link farms, as these are not normally considered for higher ranking and are most often considered spamdexing (or spamexing). Google has stated that websites or blogs participating in link farms could very likely see their search rankings penalized. You don't want to lose your ranking with Google!

- **Paid Links** – There are companies out there on the internet who will link to you, for a price. This is normally inexpensive, but can to be fatal. Major search engines look very poorly at websites who sell links and at those sites paying for the back link. Best to avoid.

What's a "Good" backlink?

The answer to this is simple. Genuine links between sites with related content. This will boost your page rank with search engines! Contribute to the internet by writing quality content. If your content is good quality, other site will be eager to link back to you. You also need to link back to others with related and quality content.

If you want top search engine rankings, you need to play by the their rules. You can use sneaky little tricks to get rankings, but, at some point, you will be found out and lose those rankings. It's a lot of work, but much better to build your page rank the correct way and keep your standing.

Getting quality backlinks should be your goal. This may be a little difficult at first because website owners may be reluctant to link to you. The reason for their reluctance is simple. If a quality website links to too many lower quality site, their own search engine ranking could be hurt.

You can check your ranking and the ranking of other websites by using tools like PRChecker.

How to Generate Good Backlinks

There are two really great ways to get the quality backlinks you need.

- First, be sure to write quality content on your blog or website. With quality content, other sites will want to link to you.

- Second, get involved on the web. Participate in forums, leave comments, participate on discussion boards, add to threads and leave comments on other blog posts. Always include a link back to your blog. **DO NOT SPAM**!

Now having said all that, let me tell you the easiest and quickest way to get quality backlinks. Leave quality comments on related blog posts. These comments must be quality. Not just "great post" with your link, this is not a quality comment. Add to the discussion. Share some of your knowledge or experience. Others will read your comment and click on your link to see what else you have to say.

If you've written a blog post that relates to the blog where you'd like to leave a comment, include the link to that blog post in your comment. You can build significant traffic by contributing to the internet in a useful manner.

SEO Scams

Be very careful. There is no SEO magic bullet that can guarantee you will get top organic search results. A lot of companies out there are making promises they can't keep and are eager to separate you from your money.

Quality SEO work is available, but it's a lot of hard work and isn't cheap. It requires tweaking every page of your website, submitting your website/blog to all search engines, submitting articles and press releases, all on a regular basis.

The term organic search results means that you haven't paid for an ad placement. If you hire a company, be sure they aren't posting to unrelated sites or using paid links to bolster their results. Scamming people with fake results is very easy.

Don't Forget to Promote Your Blog

If the blog is for your friends and family or personal use only, promoting really isn't necessary. However, if you're blogging about your business and/or products, promotion of your blog is essential.

The most important thing you can do is write good content and write often. When someone comes to your blog, they should have the choice to read several different blogging posts. If your content is weak, or you only have a couple of posts, there's no reason for them to return. Writing daily is a good idea, but if not daily, at least a few times a week.

It would be wise to wait a least a month before actively promoting your blog. This will give you the chance to create several high quality posts, thus giving your visitor something to read and a reason to return.

Another key promotion tips is to email all your friend and relatives and ask them to visit your blog. Do some self-promoting. Ask for their input, that way they won't be able to resist visiting your blog. Everyone loves to give his or her opinion!

There are numerous FREE ways to promote your blog. Here are just a few to get your started:

- Leave unique or **useful** comments on other blogs, humor is always good.
- Write a guest post for another blog
- Exchange links with other bloggers

- Start a second blog and link to the original one (but only after you get the first one running well)
- Email your friends, family and contacts with new blog posts that may interest them. Ask them to share with friends.
- Use social networks such as Facebook, MySpace, Twitter and YouTube. Join every social network you can.
- Join MyBlogLog.com or BlogCatalog.com
- Place a Stumble Button in your post template
- Submit your blog to blog directories or blog search engines such as:
  o Syndic8
  o FeedPlex
  o Technorati
  o RSS Network
- Email other bloggers and introduce yourself
- Convert blog posts to PDF files and submit them to Scribd.com – be sure to include your blog URL in the description and in document itself.
- Write a review on Amazon and eBay
- Put links in your current postings referring back to older posts. Be sure to create text links. These links need to be descriptive, do not use "click here". Search Engine Spiders search text links in order to rank your post; "click here" is pretty useless. An example of how a text link should look would be

something like, "Check out my previous post on <u>Bathing Your Cat</u>". "Bathing Your Cat' would be the text link. If you want to know how to give your cat a bath, are you going to type "click here" in the search bar or will you type in something more related such as "Bathing your cat"?

- Search for forums in your niche and answer whatever questions people may have.

- Check into using Wikio. This is a news website that you can personalize to suite your interests. This site allows you to create pages for following breaking news on topics of your choice. You can comment on existing items or publish your own commentary.

- Write articles about your subject matter and post them on article sites.

- Write a press release. This is a perfect way of announcing your blog and its content to the world. Below are a few free Press Release sites. When you get ready to submit, it's wise to do a search online for current information on free press release websites:

  o <u>www.i-newswire.com</u>

  o <u>www.openpr.com</u>

  o <u>www.prlog.org</u>

Remember to always have a link to your blog in your signature line. This is very important when you do any of the things on the list above. What's the point of leaving comments on other peoples posts or being a guest blogger, if the readers can't find you?

No link, no traffic and traffic is the whole point!

When you're ready to spend some serious time promoting your blog, you can look online for more ideas. I've seen articles with over 100 ideas for promoting your blog. This list barely scratches the surface, but will get your started.

How to Make Money with Your Blog

There are many bloggers today who do make money online with their blogs. They run these blogs like a business and make a decent living. However, not every blog is going to be a moneymaker.

Blogs can make you money through both direct and indirect income methods. Selling items on your blog, such as mugs, pens, tee shirts, etc. would be a considered a direct income method, while posting affiliate banners and links or advertising for other companies, would be an examples of indirect methods.

Selling Advertising on Your Blog

Bloggers who are also entrepreneurs tend to use two major types of blogging techniques to make money by advertising businesses on their blogs. The most popular method is to turn your blog into a moneymaking machine by selling advertising to companies with items of interest to your readers. The second method is to sell advertising to a single brand to improve its image. Creating a positive association in your readers mind accomplishes this goal.

Either method can be a great way for making you money, especially if you have marketing knowledge and/or sales experience.

There's numerous ways you could conceivability sell advertising, but the following two basic methods are used most often.

One method you can use is to actively recruit sponsors who have products of interest to your readers. You can do this yourself, or if you don't have the time but you have the budget, you can hire someone else to contact these companies for you. At least in the beginning, to get you started, taking advantage of programs like Google's AdSense, can save you a considerable amount of time and effort. These programs may require less effort on your part, but you may make less money then what you imagined. However, still not a bad idea until you can get other advertisers to agree to partner with you.

The most lucrative way, by far, is to sell advertising directly to companies. This method is much easier for people with a strong background in sales and who have experience presenting their ideas to others. Convincing companies to put links or banners on your blog can be very time consuming. However, you do stand to make quite a bit of money using this method. One drawback is that before you can hope to attract most advertisers, you'd need to have a large readership. It can possibly take you several months of blogging before you could accomplish this. If you're lucky enough to have contacts within the companies you'd like on your blog, you can cut the time down considerably.

One thing to your advantage is that many companies have recognizing the popularity of blogs and the benefits of placing their advertising on them. Numerous companies are even creating their own blogs to appeal to their customer base and create a positive public image. Companies have been known to approach bloggers and ask them to design a blog for them. This can definitely prove to be a very profitable endeavor for the lucky blogger.

Affiliate Income

This can be an interesting and lucrative way to make money with your blog. An affiliate program works by offering you a commission to send your readers to their website. If your reader becomes a buyer you'll receive a percentage of the sale, or a set amount, depending on how the program is set up.

Choose affiliates that are offering products and services related to the topic or topics discussed in your blog. Your readers are a target audience, which means targeted traffic for your affiliate. They're reading your blog because they already have an interest in the subject matter, therefore it only makes sense they'd be interested in the product offered by your affiliate.

There are thousands of affiliates programs out there to choose from. You shouldn't have any trouble finding one, or several that are a perfect fit for your particular blog content.

Also, it's a good idea to blog occasionally about your affiliates and what they offer, so you may want to really believe in what they're product or service.

Speaking Invitations

It isn't uncommon for people to read blogs, scouting for a speaker. They may need someone to speak at a workshop or seminar. Many will offer to pay you for your services, although others may ask you to speak for free. Think carefully before turning down a gratis invitation to speak. This is an opportunity to get your message, and name, in front of a live audience, creating more interest in your blog and adding to your credibility. This can bring many more opportunities your way.

Subscription Based Blogs

If you're a highly regarded expert in your field, this method may work for you. But remember, people can find all types of information on the web for free, so you really need to have something unique to offer.

Selling Items on Your Blog

Another way, you can make some money with your blog, is to sell tee shirts, pins, cups, pens, or anything that can be personalized. Create your own logo and post it in your blog design, that way when you get a large, loyal following, you can sell these small, personalized items. This will make your readers feel connected to their online family.

Selling the Blogs Themselves

Once your blog acquires a large readership, you can offer it for sale. Most people prefer to sell their blogs on auctions sites. Expect perspective buyers to go and check out your blog, the number of visitors you receive, and the quality of your posts, before they place a bid.

Blogs with quality content and a large audience will create the most interest and as a result, they'll bring a higher selling price. If you sell a quality website associated with the blog, as a package deal, you may be surprised at the amount of money it'll bring at auction.

Sell Your Skills

Once your blog has proven to be a success, containing quality, well written content and with a large, loyal following, you could start to receive offers to write for others. Some people may want to hire you to write articles for their websites. Others might like your style and ask you to freelance for them, writing for a newspaper or magazine. The big thing to remember here is that your reputation is going to be very important. Don't do anything to tarnish it. Remember that with every post you write.

More on Affiliate Marketing

As mentioned previously, affiliate marketing can be a great way to generate revenue on your blog. Essentially, affiliate marketing requires you to create a link or banner on your blog to the affiliates website. Contacts vary by affiliate as to what the requirements are to receive compensation. They may offer compensation each time the link receives a click, others will require a purchase, while some will require the visitor to register with the affiliate website.

Selecting an Affiliate Opportunity

Numerous opportunities are available in affiliate marketing. All types of websites and companies participate in this type of marketing. Be very careful when selecting the companies or websites with which you'd like to be affiliated. Keep your target audience in mind. Just because you managed to get a great affiliate contract with a knitting website, it won't do you any good if your blog content is centered on the outdoor sportsman. For successful affiliate marketing, pick websites or companies who complement your blog and are not in direct competition with it. This will help to ensure that your blog visitors will find the link interesting and not annoying.

Requirements Associated with Affiliate Marketing

Read the agreement carefully before requesting to be an affiliate. For example, some companies may restrict you from placing an affiliate link on the same blog with a competitor's link or advertisement. While others have guidelines as to what they feel is objectionable content. If you fail to adhere to their guidelines, you could not only lose your privileges with the affiliate, but also be denied compensation.

Be clear on how you'll be paid. Do you need to have a PayPal account in order to receive your commissions? Or will they deposit it into your bank account? Are they going to send you a check? How often will you be paid? Every week, twice a month, once a month or will you be paid on a quarterly basis? What is required for you to be paid? Will your visitor need to purchase something? Do they sign up for the site? How much is your commission? Is it a percentage of the purchase, or is it a set amount?

If you don't like the requirements or compensation plan, look for another affiliate. You're going to be posting a link or banner and blogging about the business or service, so make it worth your time. There's so many out there, it isn't necessary to settle for one that doesn't meet your needs.

Submitting to an Affiliate

The process for submitting to an affiliate for acceptance is relatively simple. You'll need to submit the website address of your blog and fill out the required information online to be approved. Normally the information required is pretty standard, such as name, address, email address and maybe your PayPal email address. Companies or websites will normally approve your application pretty quickly, unless of course, your blog is deemed to be in conflict with the company's goals or contains material their guidelines outline as objectionable.

Maximizing Opportunities on Affiliate Marketing

You've selected an affiliate marketing opportunity, so now what?

First and foremost, do everything you can to bring traffic to your blog. Use all your promotion techniques to bring in as many visitors, new and previous, as possible.

Create and post some blog content concerning the affiliate company's product or service. Create some interest in your readers so they'll want to click on the link, or banner, to check out the offer.

Evaluate the effectiveness of the link or banner you're using. How many visitors has your blog received in a certain timeframe? How many clicked on the link? If your percentage of clicks per visitors is very small, you may want to consider repositioning the link or banner. Maybe the banner is too small, or just isn't very appealing. Try changing the location and recheck your data again in a week or two. If that worked, great! If not, then give the banner a facelift and check traffic again in an allotted period of time.

Whatever changes you make, do them one at a time, so you can accurately judge what change had the desired affect. Be sure to make this evaluation on a regular basis. You need to continue to keep on top of this and make any changes that are necessary.

Video Blogging (or Vlogging)

Video on the web is nothing new. Now that video equipment can be purchased for a reasonable cost, video blogging has become very popular worldwide. Anymore, video-editing software is relatively easy to use. In no time, you can create, edit and post a **simple** video online. However, it can be time consuming to produce a video with worthwhile content.

There are advantages, as well as disadvantages to video blogging. A video blog can create an exciting user experience, which can have a very positive influence on the amount of traffic coming to your blog. On the other hand, it takes more time to create and search engines are not able to read it for content.

Making a Good Video Blog

Probably the most important thing to remember when creating a video blog is to cover topics that interest you and that you have a passion for.

It's just as important in a video blog as it is in a written blog to draw the visitor in immediately. Capture them with your first few sentences, or you may lose them.

You have a very limited amount of time to catch their attention. When you do get their attention, don't let your story lag, keep it flowing and above all, be concise.

Keep in mind the attention span of your audience. Don't go on too long. Get to the point. If you have several points you'd like to cover, make several videos and post them a few days apart. This will allow you to go into detail on each point and not loose your visitors. You'll create excitement and they'll want to hear the next point. This will create traffic to your blog.

When filming, be sure your picture is clear, not fuzzy. No one wants to watch something out of focus.

Good lighting is a must; don't you just hate movies where you can't see what's going on?

Pay attention to the quality of the audio, also. Static is not a pleasant sound and it distracts from the message.

Post quality videos. Take some time to create an outline in your mind on what you want to accomplish, before you begin.

Watch your videos. What can you do to improve on the next one? Always look for ways to improve the quality of the picture or audio, don't forget to consider improving the content.

Remember, to just be yourself and it'll get easier every time you make one. So just preserve and you can find success in this blogging medium.

Video Blogging Advantages

Videos generate an excitement for the blog visitor, successfully grabbing their attention and keeping it. Dynamic content in a video will create much more excitement than the same content when it's written. When you create a more enthusiastic viewer, the quicker word will spread about your blog and the more traffic you'll receive. They'll tell everyone about the great blog they've found.

Video blogs are fun to make; this creates a positive experience for you. If you enjoy creating something, you'll do it on a more regular basis.

Video Blogging Disadvantages

One obvious disadvantage is the time it takes to create and upload a video. You can certainly write a text post in significantly less time. You'll need to consider the amount of time you have to dedicate to this project.

Video blog content isn't searchable by search engine spiders, which can make your blog a little more difficult to find. You can work around this by posting some text as well, perhaps giving your readers an overview of what they're about to see in the video.

One real problem is that video blogs can be very slow to load for some viewers, causing frustration for your blog visitors. Many people will move to another blog, rather than wait for your video to load.

Post Regularly

Just as with a text blog, posting regularly is very important. You must continually create new videos. If you don't add new content to your video blog on a regular basis, people will lose interest and no long visit your blog.

Creating new video content can be very time consuming if done one at a time, on an as needed basis. For the best use of your time, you can create several videos at one time. You may have to spend a whole day doing this, but it'll save you time in the long run. After you've created all the videos for that week (month), you can space them out when uploading them to your site. Spend one day a week creating your videos and the rest of the week posting them.

Be sure you create videos on a subject that will interest others or on something they may want to learn. A video on watching grass grow will probably not create a lot of buzz or return traffic.

The whole point is to keep your blog visitors happy. This way they'll continue to return and tell their friends and family about you. By creating continuous traffic to your blog, and making those visitors want to return, you will ensure your blog is successful.

Autoblogging

Autoblogging is using different types of programs to search the web for blog content, then posting that content to your blog. Many feel this is a type of "stealing", while others feel it makes perfect sense.

Many businesses, such as News Relay Services, Real Estate Agents and even recipe blogs feel this method save them countless hours of work. They can pull fresh content from the web and have it automatically posted to their blog. They consider it a valuable asset to their business.

I'm presenting this technique to you, so you can make your own decision as to whether or not you want to use it for your blog. One thing I must mention here is that before adding a feed, you need to be sure there are no copyright violations.

Install WordPress

Your first step is to install WordPress. This is a very flexible and free blogging package. You can download WordPress by doing a search on the web. Many hosting companies provide it as part of your hosting package and it's normally very easy to install.

Install Plugins

WordPress has many types of plugins that perform various functions for you. The following list contains a few of the plugins you may want to download.

- FeedWordPress – Allows WordPress to import RSS feeds from the internet

- WP Auto Tagger – Cuts down the work you'll need to do on each post by automatically adding the keywords for you.

- Delete Duplicate Posts – You'll need this plugin to make sure your database doesn't contain duplicate posts.

- WP O-Matic – This WordPress plugin permits the blogger to automatically create posts from feeds. It provides a simple interface so the blogger can type in the feed URL. You would then select the category where the post is to be created. Multiple feed and categories are possible. You'll also be able to write your own posts in each category.

More plugins that might interest you:

- Google XML Sitemaps
- Google Analyticator
- KeywordLuv
- SEO Smart Links
- SEO friendly Images
- WP Auto Tagger
- WordPress MU – For multiple sites

There are numerous plugins available. You'll need to decide which ones make sense for your blog.

Setting Up Your Feeds

After you've installed your plugins in WordPress and your blog in up and running, you'll need to add feeds. As an example, you may want to add a feed from Google. To do this you'd follow these steps:

- First go to http://blogsearch.google.com
- Do a search relating to your blog content. Let's say your blog will be dedicated to Motorcycle Rallies, type in Motorcycle Rallies. Take a look at the results to be sure is the type of information you want.

- In the left hand column, there's a link for RSS. Right click (or Control click for Mac) on RSS. A menu will appear allowing you to "copy link". Our link for this example looks like this: http://blogsearch.google.com/blogsearch_feeds?hl=en&q=motorcycle+rallies&ie=utf-8&num=10&output=rss

- Paste this link into FeedWordPress. Now your website or blog will scan the blogshere, on a schedule you've determined, looking for new post related to your topic.

Managing Posts

FeedWordPress will ask you at set-up if you'd like posts to be posted or held for moderation. Until you become familiar with the system, it's best to hold your posts for moderation.

WordPress allows for advanced functions to be built into your website or blog. You'll want to check out all the scripts available to see which ones will suite your needs best.

Scripts will automate parts of the process for you. Some scan new posts for content, while others will delete or skip items.

This is an example of a simple script that runs a WordPress function every 15 minutes.

```
[source                    lang="php"]$wpdb->query("UPDATE
`www_greatchefs_com`.`wp_posts` SET `post_date` = '".date('Y-
m-d                                    H:i:s')."',
`post_date_gmt`      =      '".date('Y-m-d      H:i:s')."',
`post_modified`      =      '".date('Y-m-d      H:i:s')."',
`post_modified_gmt`  =  '".date('Y-m-d  H:i:s')."'  WHERE
`post_date`          <          '2000-01-01          00:00:00';
");
[/source]
```

What this script does is look for any post with a date prior to January 1, 2002. When it finds one, it automatically updates the post with the current date.

Final Steps

This step takes away the true autoblogging concept, because it requires human intervention. You don't need to do this, but it's a good idea.

Do a final scan of each article to be posted to ensure it's accurate. This way you ensure your target audience is getting the correct information.

Mobile Blogging (Moblogs)

Mobile blogging is spreading like wildfire! This method allows bloggers to create posts on the run, making it extremely convenient to create repeated updates to their blogs and keep the content fresh for their visitors.

Mobile blogging devices allow bloggers to post current and original content from nearly anywhere in the world. People are able to post to their blogs as an event is happening. There's no need to get your computer out and log on to create your posts.

In the last couple of years, mobile web devices have become so user friendly, that nearly anyone can use them effectively. Coupled with the camera's that are now standard on most phones, bloggers are able to get out into the world and keep visitors updated on events, as they happen.

With mobile web devices becoming less expensive and mobile blogging becoming so widespread, it's conceivable that moblogs will become the dominant blogging method of the future. It's easy to imagine a future with bloggers updating their blogs with imagines and text as an event is actually happening. This was a privilege currently reserved for journalists and the news media.

Because Mobile blogging can be done anywhere and anytime, it's definitely a trend to watch.

How to Manage Multiple Blogs

Many feel that maintaining one blog is enough work, but there are many bloggers who choose to manage several blogs at one time. This is difficult for a lot of bloggers, but if you're someone who'd like to give it a try, here are a few tips that should be able to help.

How do You Find Time for Each Blog

This is possibly the biggest reason multiple blogs fail. Unless you have absolutely no life, you are going to have other interest that put demands on your time. After all, there are only so many hours in a day.

If you're doing to have more than one blog, you can't ignore one and work extra on another one. You have to a lot time for each of them; otherwise you're going to loss the valuable traffic you worked so hard to get.

Time management will be essential here. You would be well advised to set up an actual schedule and stick to it. Of course, all blog topics won't require the same amount of time, so you'll need to allot your time accordingly. You'll need to assess your blog traffic and comments; to be sure none of your blogs are suffering. When you see issues arising, you may want to consider asking someone to help you or eliminating a blog altogether.

Each Blog Needs Original Content

This is very important. You need to keep each blog original and fresh. Be careful not to post similar information on more than one blog. Not only is this a waste of time for you, but also your visitors will drift away or begin visiting only one of your blogs. There'd be no need for them to visit the blog with reworded content.

One thing you never want to do is steal content from another blogger. Your readers will notice at some point and stop following you. It's great to read other blogs to get ideas for content, but don't copy them. Build on what they have to say. For example, say you find a blog with 10 gardening tips, take 2 or 3 of those tips and build on them. You can create a blog post expounding on a single tip. Then create another complete post form the second tip. This may take some research for you to be able to write something in detail on a single tip. But you can be sure there are people out there who would like complete details.

Each Blog Must be Kept Up To Date

You'll need to post to each blog on a regular basis. Again, you may want to set up a schedule in order to keep track of this. Don't allow your blogs to get stagnate; this will cause you to lose traffic. If you don't provide fresh content regularly, your visitors will move on to a blogger who shares your niche and is able to provide them with what they want.

Bloggers Block, Now What?

You sit there, hands on the keyboard and nothing happens! Nothing! Your mind is a complete blank. You know you HAVE to post fresh content to your blog, but you have nothing, not a word. The more you try to think of something, the worse it gets. Normally your mind runs wild with ideas, but all the sudden you feel like you're trying to function in a vacuum. This happens to everyone from time to time, the trick is to not let yourself get stuck there for too long.

Don't worry; there are ways to get past this little setback. Here are a few simple tricks that should enable you to break through that bloggers block and come up with some great ideas for your blog. You just need to give your mind a kick-start.

Visit Other Blogs

This is a great idea for two reasons; first you could read something that really sparks some fresh, new ideas for you. Second, you aren't doing anything anyway, so rather than to just sit there frustrated, you may learn something new and exciting. Give it a try, you have nothing to lose.

Comment on Other Blogs

Just commenting on someone else's blog may be enough to create ideas. If you've post something to someone else's blog, there's no reason you couldn't expand on that idea and add it to your own blog.

Besides, commenting will put your name out there. Don't forget to put that all too important signature tag, containing your blogs address, in your signature line. Others may be interested in your comment and want to check out your blog, thus creating traffic for yourself.

Check Out Your Own Blogs' Comments

Someone may make a comment, which will spur an idea. Are they asking a question you can answer by creating another blog post? Did they bring up a point you hadn't covered? You can add a post expounding on that point. If they have a link to their blog, go check it out. You may get some fresh ideas by reading their blog posts.

Check Your Blogs' Email

Check out the email address for your blog. What do people have to say? Again, did they ask a question? Can you make that into a blog post?

Read Some Articles Online or in Magazines

Do a search for articles written concerning your niche. Reach some articles and see if they give you a fresh perspective on your topic. Magazines are great for gaining new insight on your niche

Watch the Evening News

Who knows, there may be something related to your subject matter. Even if it isn't directly related, you may find a way of connecting an event to your topic. There's always something happening in the world , so you will always have a source of material.

The avenues to come up with fresh material are numerous, but these few should at least get you moving and initiate some new ideas. Just changing your focus off the task of writing your blog and putting it into researching your topic, can be enough to create a new point of view.

Now kiss that bloggers block good-bye and start writing again!

A Few Reasons That Can Cause a Blog to Fail

Many people start new blogs every day. Unfortunately, many of them will fail. Many times the reason for the failure of their blog is 100% preventable. Below is a list of several of the main reasons that can cause a blog to fail.

Wrong Niche

If your blog is for personal reasons only, the niche you pick isn't really all that relevant. You're blogging for family, friends, or maybe just yourself in a personal blog.

However, if you're blogging to make money, traffic is extremely important, so don't underestimate the simple concept of "Supply and Demand". People will have to want to actually read what you have to write.

If you think that you've found the perfect niche because no one else out there on the web is writing about it in his or her blog; you're probably going to be disappointed. The reason there's no blog is probably because no one out there is interested in the topic.

Lack of Focus

You started off just great! You had a topic for your blog and you posted relevant information. Then somewhere along the way, you started to verbally wander. Now your blog doesn't even touch on your original theme. You've wandered off verbally into another topic, or maybe just began rambling.

Your posts are completely unrelated. You've lost your readers. All that hard won traffic has found someone else's blog to read. Now they're following a person who stays on topic and is posting relevant and interesting information.

Not Posting Original Posts

Copying someone else's blog posts can spell certain death for your blog. You're visitors are looking at other blogs on the web, that are related to your topic. They will notice if you're copying someone else. Do Not Copy for other bloggers.

Assuming "Get Rich Quick"

If you think for a moment all you need to do is post some content and you're going to get rich overnight, you're going to be sorely disappointed!

A successful, moneymaking blog can take weeks, even months before it starts to make you a decent income. It's going to take hard work, lots of original and interesting posts, dedication and a lot of time to be a success. There's no real reason you can't do it, if you're willing to put the work into it.

While you're waiting for your blog to build those all-important visitors and subscribers, spend some time getting to know your readers. Read their comments and pay attention to what's important to them.

Blogger has Too Many Blogs

Another way to fail is by starting too many blogs at one time. It's wise to get one blog up and going, showing success, before you start thinking about starting another one. Give one blog your full attention; make it a success before beginning you next project.

Having No Credibility

Don't pretend to be an expert on something, if you aren't. Once you lose your credibility, it's nearly impossible to build it back again. Be real and be yourself.

It's perfectly acceptable to talk about a topic and not be an expert, just share what you know and/or what you're learning. Many times people are not only looking to read blogs discussing how to be successful, they also want to know what NOT to do. They don't want to fail, so share your failures and successes. They'll enjoy reading both and this will give them the opportunity to learn not only from your successes but also from your mistakes. Hopefully they can avoid making the same mistakes themselves.

Even though this list is not an all-inclusive list of reasons for blog failure, it is a list of the major causes bloggers aren't successful. If you avoid making these mistakes, at least you'll have a head start at producing a success blog for yourself and your readers.

Basic Steps to Begin Your Blog

In conclusion, these are the basic steps you need to take to begin your blogging career. By following these steps you can get a blog up and running in no time at all.

- Decide what type of blog you want to create
    - Personal
    - Business
    - Cause
    - Educational
- Choose a topic/niche (for a personal blog, this isn't necessary)
- Research your topic (for a personal blog, this isn't necessary)
- Find the blogging site you'd like to use
- Set up and personalize your template
- Write your first post
- Keep creating posts and post regularly

For a personal blog the following two steps are unnecessary:

- Follow Search Engine Optimization (SEO) strategies
- Promote your Blog

If you're creating a personal blog, you can literally have your blog up and running in about 15 minutes!

A business blog, or one created for the purpose of making money through affiliate marketing, will take more time, due to the extra steps involved.

You may want to devote some time upfront to doing research, if you need to decide on a niche that will work well for you.

Benjamin Franklin once said, *"All things come to he who waits."*

However, several years ago I saw a variation of this quote I liked much better; *"He who waits ends up waiting."*

So quit waiting, and get started!